Man & Beast

Man & Beast

Eric Cole

A 4 A.M. BOOK

INSOMNIAC PRESS

Copyright © 2005 by Eric Cole

All rights reserved. No part of this publication may be reproduced, stored in a retrieval system or transmitted, in any form or by any means, without the prior written permission of the publisher or, in case of photocopying or other reprographic copying, a license from Access Copyright, 1 Yonge Street, Suite 1900, Toronto, Ontario, Canada, M5E 1E5.

Library and Archives Canada Cataloguing in Publication

Cole, Eric, 1959-
  Man & beast / Eric Cole.

Poems.
ISBN 1-897178-04-2

1. Animals--Poetry. I. Title.

PR6103.O54M36 2005   821'.92   C2005-904439-X

The publisher gratefully acknowledges the support of the Canada Council, the Ontario Arts Council and the Department of Canadian Heritage through the Book Publishing Industry Development Program.

Printed and bound in Canada
Insomniac Press
192 Spadina Avenue, Suite 403
Toronto, Ontario, Canada, M5T 2C2
www.insomniacpress.com

This book is dedicated to my mother, Angela.

Contents

I
Man ... 11

Adam's Prayer ... 13
The Apple-Namer ... 14
Ringmaster ... 15
Mackerel Man ... 16
The Brothers ... 17
Students ... 18
Cuchulain Dies ... 20
Armada ... 21
Rhino Keeper ... 22
Moving Statues ... 23
Fairy-Ring ... 24
Lough Derg ... 25
Greece ... 26
Another World ... 27
Indian Summer ... 28
Bus Journey ... 30
Unemployed ... 31
Pine-Falls Winter ... 32
Sasquatch ... 33
Phil ... 34
The Connoisseur of Moose Mountain Speaks ... 35
The Worm-Pickers ... 36
Chuck ... 37

Wounded Knee	38
Death of a Poet	39
Yobi	40
The Plumber	41
Roadkill	42
The Senile Birdwatcher	43

2
Meet the Hairy-Nosed Wombat Keeper	45
Meet the Hairy-Nosed Wombat Keeper	47

3
Beast	49
Butterflies	51
Octopus	52
Starfish	53
Zebra Mussels	54
Portugese Man O' War	55
Tuna	56
Frogs	57
Snapping Turtle	58
Snake	59
Tortoise	60
Dinosaurs	61
Rail	62
Cowbirds	63

Chicken	64
Hyacinth Macaw	65
Siberian Crane Dance	66
Blackpoll Warbler	68
King Penguin	69
Echidna	70
Elephant Shrew	71
Mole	72
Kangaroo	73
Hedgehog	74
Sloth	75
Pangolin	76
Beaver	77
Grey-Headed Flying Fox	78
Aardvark	79
Snowshoe Hare	80
Badger	81
Red Panda	82
Warthog	83
Musk Ox	84
Zebra	85
Hippo	86
Rhino	87
Hyena	88
Black Bear	89
Snow Leopard	90
Grey Seal	91
Sea Cows	92

Elephants	93
Right Whale	96
Gibbon	97
Chimpanzee	98
Notes	99
Acknowledgements	107

1
Man

ADAM'S PRAYER

They will argue my rib from the earliest mountain
and dig for the places where God's half-dreamed angels
came down to instruct me on fathering saints,
on the menus of men and the uses of Eve,
and how among that falling fruit, we heard
the snarls of first animals losing their souls.
All life on the lip of Eden being eaten
would come to pass with my sinner sons,
their taste for sacrifice, transcribing dreams,
running rampant, epileptic, surged
to desert ends, abandonment of age.
My God, my time, five dogs beyond
that first tight succulence of Eve,
give strength to the stick I shake at her seed.

The Apple-Namer

A year since my wife dreamed she was a sick pigeon,
her toes have turned inwards, she nods more frequently.
I have marked the increased preference for grain.
In her dreams now she has to flap her arms ever more rapidly
just to make it above the trees. Sometimes destitution
on pavement with people tossing her crumbs
will startle her from sleep. I live with this nonsense,
my reputation as an apple-namer is at stake;
there's Granny Smith, McIntosh, Golden Delicious to better.
Each day *I* fly off the handle at clients
who just won't accept that all the good names are gone.
Each day I find more feathers on her pillow...
After a year she's a very sick pigeon.

RINGMASTER

Wind sharpens the waste-ground, a tiger coughs.
Through reluctance we lean the jaded tent upright.
By midnight the elephant-generator has hauled
a rumbling heat through the crust of bunched trailers
where candles from the Eastern-Bloc
protein the faces with gypsy-fangs
of freak and magician, hunched over cards,
with the dwarf trapeze-catcher who doubles as clown.
Sleep tricks and eludes, the latest petition
alleges cruelty and demands our function.
No longer fond or exotic ancestry,
what are we now that used to close the stars with straw?
Tomorrow, in the spotlight of a ragged ark
I will hold the world back, with a chair and a whip.

MACKEREL MAN

The light pours into evenings' whiskey stares.
Uncounted too the easy autumns,
passing fish for coins on Friday's corner,
a measure of sympathy in each exchange.
But what are hands without the needs of a town?
No pocket fits their land, no woman wants
a moment of their touch. All that is gone,
and I remain as huge and odd, a friend to boys
who love small fights of mackerel on a line.
Alone I fish the rising tide beyond
where the promenade's lights lick the naked bathers,
romping after the disco, drunk. Their cold
penetration grips the oars. I gut my catch,
take the sweet roe on a knife to my mouth.

THE BROTHERS

The Brothers went through generations of boys.
Irish knives through Irish butter. Wielding
saints' names like sceptres didn't stop
our using the more apt nick-names they'd earned.
Taskmasters of Christ and Country doled out
the perfect mix of intimidation and affection.
Woe betide you rub "Wally" up the wrong way,
so proficient with the strap he made "Rasher" look like
an amateur reddening as he walloped with his cane.
"Cats" stalked from behind, bestowed his 'applause'
on both sides of any head not bent on its lessons.
Heads that years later enrolled their only sons,
trusting their futures to the hands of their past,
men of the collar on a long leash from God.

STUDENTS

I

In our tent rivulets breached our dams of dirty clothes
to seep into the clean ones we'd piled up as our pillows.
Le castration de la maize, rain-delayed for weeks,
held encamped a student workforce with a multicultural fuse.
When Witindi Kambali, a Zairean math scholar
carried his belongings on his head and figured out
how to stay dry, a mob burned down the toilets.
The Syrian faction blamed the Lebanese,
but they all loved the Irish because we weren't English.
Knives appeared from under saris, wet pyjamas,
tearing hunks from spitted lambs they sent to sooth us.
Witindi Kambali said "'tis good, 'tis sweet"
after eating a locust in the seething discontent,
the constant rain, the fault of the French.

2

When John Paul 1 died we were in the maize,
castrating away, rendering it celibate. A storm,
worthy of a pope-death, deflowered on our heads.
We tied our feet in plastic bags, danced a jig at heaven.
The mad farmer's wife was a tad retarded,
as an orphan she used to gnaw at his turnips.
As punishment he married her. She giggled
when he dragged me to her room, he claimed
the last Irish lads got chicken pox from screwing
his chickens, and this would divert me from that.
Later, hitching to the Pyrenees, I learned the gays
were the ones who stopped even when you weren't hitching.
Suddenly Jesus was everywhere, and his mother in bottles,
but visiting Lourdes had no cure for my ills.

CUCHULAIN DIES

I hear the sea, all horse and long retreated
come under otters, lapping for my blood.
What sport for deer, that flight of spears I caught,
that all around my feet fowl broods of swans,
my bowels, I gathered up and staggered here,
to lash against this pillar, final youth...
A life of severed heads and friendship shortened
to bloody myth. Where are you now wild Fergus?
Maeve's shaggy host is dashing forth from Connaught
as Ulster's witches languish under solstice.
Before me, Druids call down the immediate stars,
to pierce my light and cast my grip in stone.
The endings are closing that are older than ghosts,
the raven's wing-beats batter to my heart.

ARMADA

The gale made soggy wool of us all,
in trails of coarse shawl ragged to the shore,
where the wreckage, spilling Spaniards, groaned,
and cheers for plunder rose among the gathered.
Some came prepared, McCabb was in the surf,
welcoming the half-dead with an axe.
Some said gold and billowing silk
had pulled the sons of The Escorial under,
and I, a mother, wept, mothering hope
that God would deliver them in later tides.
More crawled ashore, we leapt like sheep on sheep
helping or stripping with a flair that English soldiers
mocked as our savagery, then jostled us back,
turning their sabers to methodical slaughter.

RHINO KEEPER

When the rhinos were ridin' at the Dublin Zoo
one ould one gigglin' said *his* looked like the Concord,
comparin' it to her man's. Corus Iompar Eireann,
proud sponsors, enquired if you please, when the calf was due.
The date of arrival was posted on the rail.
By then please God, me golden handshake
will shake me dust where forty years
slap-a-rhino's been my whack at the world
and it wasn't Jasus easy either,
wha' with young ones watchin', turnin' Africa's tonnage
on a finger an' snortin' an inch from me bollicks
that horn them poachers cringe in the thorns for
on TV, where I seen also forty Roman soldiers
were needed to haul one bleedin' rhino to the Games...
be Jasus, it's a wonder I'm still alive at all.

Moving Statues

We were tracing Greek lines through Claudian sculpture,
when statues of Mary were starting to move.
In tacky grotto settings, plaster and marble
were no longer containing the Immaculate fingers.
All over Ireland holy toes were twitching,
and droves of craw-thumpers traipsed about.
The Ballinspittle criers drooled, and slapped
together bleachers for the bused-in hoards.
Student colleagues testified they saw The Virgin nod;
some saw the light of heaven shining at her head.
On the verge of a national euphoric revelation,
the signs abruptly ceased, the sacred lips re-sealed.
Some say God, like Claudius, got cold feet,
and at the last minute turned from the enraptured Irish.

FAIRY-RING

At the lake-edge small waves lapped at their feet,
wind brushed their hair, ushering them on.
They'd been this way twice, now a low moon
skimmed along the trees beside them.
By the round tower yews grapple and retreat,
the gravestones lean down to reach them.
Grabbing her hand he swore he knew the way
to the portal of Glendalough's car-park.
So a twisting path, cut by tangled brier,
fit for spooked sheep, took them on.
When they came out again to the same lake-edge,
waves were lapping, like tongues, a dead swan.
With dawn, a mist crushed the feathered clarity.
From distant rings of haze the car shimmered into view.

LOUGH DERG

Three times to Lough Derg gets you into heaven.
My mother's been four, "just to make sure, Love."
On this outpost of piety, pounded bleak
by the flayed Atlantic, the sinking incantations
of pilgrims rise up when the wind dies down.
During these lulls, you're eaten alive,
by "midgets" no less. Sharp stone beds
stay the pilgrims' barefoot course.
Dry toast ration gulped down with tea
sustains dim penitents grateful for evening.
I said to my mother "It sounds like Hell."
She said "Sure Love, Hell is *nothing*
compared to Lough Derg." Meanwhile,
she'd got concessions by amusing the priest.

GREECE

Pericles' rows of stone lions sat sentinel
over the glittering treasury at Delos.
Pouring libations at the god Apollo's birthplace,
his whispered ambition surpassed the immortal's.
We watched as this 'Island of Light' receded,
the centre of empire, where its marble gods
would fight to the last like Spartan hoplites
against the invading vegetation.
On Mykinos we bought tickets to *Paradise,*
infamous party beach inaccessible by land.
Nudists wave from promontories of *Super
Paradise,* a Mecca for gays along the same route.
Dolphins cross our bow. An aging Cockney
turns his eye on me, "You going to *Super*, mate?"

ANOTHER WORLD

Your only beef with the Gulf War
was that it came on at the same time as "Another World."
A camouflaged, cropped, articulate General pinpointed
where the smart-bombs hit. He squeezed the remote
like putty in his hand. The world's press
molded into chairs before him. If not this,
fireworks over Baghdad, or pictures of a dozen
Saddam look-alikes nodding in a bunker, was what we got.
Here, your San Pedro cactus attacked by the cat,
was earmarked to scar. Eight succulent ridges
clustered with spines, was a two-inch temptation
too much for old Wardly. There was no blood
waterless wounds crusting in the spiky air,
a dry transfusion of televised heat.

INDIAN SUMMER

I

The strangled mud and leeching swamps,
the way of snails, rose to derange
each in his furious nag of insects,
cursed burdens of liberty in Selkirk's promise.
Open water, flag and bible falling
further to decay. But now our Scottish skin
could turn its tired revolt from the uncharted West
to waver south, by tribal bush, our hunger watched.
Where keener eagles filled with breast, we ate the young
outlandish pelican and crowduck-witch
from colonies erupting in raucous priesthoods.
In broadest light, we saw the smaller waters
of our seas, engulfed by heartland, ours to claim,
arrived with steel, God's bounty to be gained.

2

The brutal deception of an Indian summer.
As if the world had tilted to the north,
the sudden cold, unbridled, had the whip
of lake and wind. Our huddled fires
held fingers to its teeth. Flesh after grass
relinquished its warm vigil to the root.
Our camp had furnished to a simmer.
Now winter hearts were bursting through the staves.
Men wept and weakened, axes locked in ice.
The sky flapped through our shelters' ribs
and saw the purgatorial tatters of dreams.
Saw too, the savages' silent assembly,
place strange food at our feet,
and vanish.

BUS JOURNEY

These low journeys are no agents of occasion,
our last goodbyes staggered around a fight of dawn drunks
then filed and given over cheap to marauding miles
and the monotonous ramblings of bravado
from a driver barking justice stuck in Brylcreem of the Fifties.
Or the pale, severe woman's insistence on confiding
how the slushing toilet action transmits a type of diaper-rash.
There's snatched-at sleep, like knots within the small hours,
outside, The Great Lakes cramped in icy metal breath.
By Wawa the air had been farted out twice,
and another all-night dinner's merging ranks of smoker's cough
overwhelm the toughest appetite, where the day-long pancakes
    curl.
We board now with evermore dog-eared obedience,
a dull incorporation, Greyhound master of our wheel.

UNEMPLOYED

So less, unemployed, gradual slugs
feed long days to nights in the genes' recess.
At forty, feeling fifty, nothing
but another's mileage, maudlin looks
from a shaving mirror anxious to keep
the rising rudiments of a life in check.
Each day I do less in the house and watch
the shreds of small sovereignties gathering dust.
Outside too, the wrongs are mounting,
a sickish cream is freezing in the trough,
that horse is history, always by the wire
when I pass by weekly with new lottery tickets,
or stop to stroke where unlikely bones protrude
and wonder when our numbers will come up.

PINE-FALLS WINTER
for Na-Na Brown

Before the brown river's whirl and churning roll
tightens to trickles and shrinks, before the ice
impounds great logs upright and the smoke-stack sets
its breath below it in aprons of vapour,
some finger of winter will nudge a tired toad
down into a hole. This will happen close to you
and to us, for no animal is closer than the toad,
no other can fill so completely a hole
with itself. Around all our houses, winters
widen weak-spots and the toads edge in,
bunching cold stones and a leathery breath
beneath our bird-feeders, from where we can watch,
the small gloved hands of a chickadee's flight
carry us through the living winter.

SASQUATCH

November noon and Christ-bright Manitoba
crackles with hoar-frost, echoes on the flat.
Ears were first to fall, then in my mouth
the teeth cracked out. But still we grew
through every thinning generation north,
turning to find a muscle missing, or a foot
filled with the implosive language of fierce cold.
Until I spoke with perfect frost and lived away
the need of talk, concocting snow
to fit the eye to northern lights and night-time sun.
Slow blend of forest marrow with vast ice
eluded men with rumours of my tracks.
And yet they come, my back against the glacier will burn,
another crucifixion on the narrow lights of science.

PHIL

Here are your instructions abbreviated, Phil:
leave elbow-hard hours in the brunt of a poem,
walk where the river's persistent syndrome flows,
exhausted entrails through the hustings.
Be fish, and cast your blunt hold, upstream fish
against the city's marvellous guidance,
to where the journey's creep and stall
is spawned in instinct's easy end.
But push on Phil, your exile's uncertain purpose,
through gauntlets, like a bullet's gasp,
through waters smoking legislation,
asking half-questions that asking half answers,
-If only the start of a hand in this.
-If only our difficulties were complete.

The Connoisseur of Moose Mountain Speaks

She hugs the road like a dream, just purrs -
even at my speeds - remember when we shot that moose,
at Moose Mountain - twenty-four minutes later
I was poppin' 'em from a two-four back at my pad.
And the broads you'll pull - believe me, I know
what I'm talkin' about - I'm a goddamn
connoisseur of broads - don't mind those equality
smart-ass feminist bitches - waste of panty space,
only talk to faggots about art for Christsake.
I'm talkin' real broads, broads that can sit down,
have a conversation without interrupting all the goddamn time,
'cos they know what you mean when you're talkin' fuel-injection.
Now you take those other goddamn lesbian types,
0 to 70 in 70 years - you know what their problem is?
—Fuel injection, amigo, a lifelong lack of fuel injection.

THE WORM-PICKERS

The valley wall's a black sheet above the creek.
Fireflies comma the night, toads fill it
with phrasing impossibly small-houred.
I blow smoke at stars...make no mistake,
life's more stylish plots slot between commercials,
not where we used to be, though nights like this
are prime-time for the worm-pickers there.
Jittered, their scanning beams hunt ground,
solemn sexless groups that trudge from battered trucks.
Occasional voice, disjointed limbs of light,
abduct the worm that's up to catch the moon.
I'd watch them with the cocked head of a robin,
this sub-culture stuck in the mud of it's dream,
plucking out accents with my distant ear.

CHUCK
for Sidonia

In toques and mitts hippopotami skate
across your baby-under-blanket, under clowns
that slump as though their cotton throats were slit.
In the glow of three portholes from a Noah's Ark night-light,
that beige and tan orang-utan has guilt stitched in his grin.
What might Big Bird be hatching as he swings above your chin?
I take you to my shoulder, we dance to Batti Batti
O Belle Masetto. If Mozart saw your face
we'd have a symphony to Joy. O little Fatty,
at four months old your head is slow to settle
on toys we shake or noises out of place.
You reach with an infant's unvaccinated trust
to the whole world as if it were a rattle for your hand,
we worry when the monitor crackles with static.

WOUNDED KNEE
for Leonard Peltier

War ponies were red pick-ups at Oglala
when agents masquerading for containment
came skidding on The Bureau's truth that far
more dangerous than a bunch of drunken Indians
was a bunch of sober Indians. All around
the beat of Crazy Horse's heart, a pitch and rise,
was like cicadas or a shimmer on The Black Hills.
From places where the white dogs lift their legs,
or moments of a ghost-dance prior to death,
rushed through the reservation's leaves to where
two agents, crouching, catching crossfire, fell,
like bundled decades, heavy in the hate
that kick men's final pleas into the wind,
that kicked out Big Foot's cough at Wounded Knee...

Death of a Poet
I.M. Dan Sullivan

Had they known the danger of poetry, the crowd
may have sipped their drinks with less nonchalance
and noticed that when his name was called to read
he placed his cigarette in the ashtray and lifted
the tremble in his fingers up into his voice.
We may have suspected the shifting and sweating,
the gradual flush as something other than nerves,
and stopped him right there, preventing the collapse.
I would have hung more on his every word—
that way I'd picture his last lucid image
instead of remembering teeth on the ground
when they carried him off on a stretcher.
The reading went on until the hospital phoned—
they didn't say Dan Sullivan had died of poetry.

YOBI
for Leo

I told my mother on the phone we were naming you Leopold.
She said *'Ah Love don't, that's a desperate name,'*
then she told everyone we were naming you Napoleon,
got her emperors mixed up, but that's not why I beat you.
I took the stick to you Leo, not because it was there—
it was innocently growing in the yard for fucksake.
I did it because the baby's yelling worsened.
Between bouts of fighting with your sister you dumped
toy after toy on the floor in a tantrum, defying—
I did it because I lost control.
To regain it I stepped outside and calmly cut a stick,
stripped it of its leaves while I listened to your anarchy,
tested its appliance on the palm of my hand,
then cold as any emperor, lavished you with justice.

THE PLUMBER

I push my potatoes, mustard and matches
in behind a plumber at the checkout lane.
He's humming a repetitive ditty from Carmen.
That's how I know he's a plumber, they all
love Carmen, addicted as they are to cleavage.
No slouch himself in that department thanks
to pants dragged down by keys enough to empty
the local lunatic asylum. Now he's dropped
them in the candy and is rummaging around.
I'm thinking, *Some plumber this, blocking the flow*.
You could pack potatoes, mustard, and matches
into that cleavage and blow your way out.
He looks up as if reading my mind. I think,
too bad Bizet only wrote one symphony.

ROADKILL

Dying winds jerk turkey vultures into grappling
for footing on the high snags of their roost.
He cranes his head above the wheel to watch
the shaky black squadron fall out above him.
A bump in the gathering dusk, then another,
doesn't slow his progress to quiet gravel roads.
He cuts his engine, kills his lights, and waits.
In the space between each passing car, the stars
erupt over ditches just quelled of frog-song.
He fills this space with garbage, empties his trailer.
Tomorrow's thermals will rise in vulture-lanes,
they'll cruise for traces of decay seeping up,
like promises to heaven leaking from the earth,
whole families of raccoons bloating on asphalt.

The Senile Birdwatcher

A mind that hovers on the fall of each thought,
or shakes in a tremolo's passage of geese,
can dive in the dip of a seedy finch. Calls
for water on the wing when his wheelchair glides
onto verandahs where he's set and left.
Beneath red blankets that cover his lap
cardinals leap in his knees for flight.
From a single cheep he used to tell a sparrow,
or pinpoint reclusive thrushes at dawn,
now when the big birds swoop down for fish
he reaches for eagle, but the word flies away.
His eye pools with signs that have settled and left;
drops a loon surfacing shakes off at dusk,
mud tracks that housed once a dandy stilt.

2
Meet the Hairy-Nosed Wombat Keeper

MEET THE HAIRY-NOSED WOMBAT KEEPER

'Its not always that glamorous being the wife of a Zookeeper,
And being the wife of the Hairy-Nosed Wombat Keeper,
Is never glamorous.
When he comes home after a hard days diggin'
My Jonny likes to unwind with a case of beer—
a severe case of beer. Unwinding that enormous thirst,
Winding and unwinding those tremendous tufts,
Until we're ankle-deep in the crumbs of yesterday's stew.
Ah Jonny, says I, in the name of the crucified Jesus,
Would you step up to the scissors with them nose-hairs of yours.
My friends, all driven off with tickled faces,
Myself, driven to distraction like Delilah,
That night my last friend left for the last time,
And Jonny layin' in a polluted stupor on the couch,
Them nose-hairs floatin' in the tide of his snores,
Accumulatin' boogers in mid-air,
And wavin' at me like tentacle fingers.
Tantalized I was, when I took a hold of me finest fabric shears,
An' hacked an' chopped the wiry bastards back.
But back they grew of course, and thicker than ever,
Out they popped like baby wombats from their burrows,
Engulfin' us again. And I'm brushed aside,
Now that the nose-hairs are in the hands
Of the Health and Safety Committee, of which
My Jonny is a member in good standing,
—Great man for the old Health and Safety, is Jonny.

But some things take precedence even over H&S, says Jonny,
Personal integrity and individual rights, to name a few.
Such processes are beyond the comprehension
Of a simple girdle like myself, of course.
Another process beyond the comprehension
Of a simple girdle like myself,
Is how, in the name of all the crucified Jesuses,
Did I ever get to meet the Hairy-Nosed Wombat Keeper.'

3
Beast

BUTTERFLIES
for Tiny

The milkweed's sucked to shrunken dugs.
the leaves are etched with toughened scars.
October's a boon in forensics. Paper-thin
residuals flap in crisp north-westerlies. Raptors
batten the shoreline with their terrible feathers.
We too, batten and flap, sifting for summer,
for small things that shrivel later to gems.

My three-year-old daughter springs from the van.
Her thin red hair's asunder in the grass-heads.
She catches wind of where the monarchs cling
like post-it notes in the stunted aspens.
Wings flash open at her bustling approach,
black sudden eyes emblazon on orange
then startle to a tremble...she finds her feet and runs.

Octopus

Pulsing through the loose bag of his tricks
an octopus melted into a rock. Goggled
teens were after bigger fish, their flippers
pushed their spear-guns within range.
Each time they raised a squirming prize, yells rose
from friends on shore. A fetid ribbon
of scum the length of a week continued to keep
all but the hardiest swimmers on the beach.
The Mediterranean's cocktailed waste
defied containment—it oozed and clung.
On the last day a storm lashed the Costa Del Sol
coating the wreaked beach furniture with slime,
tossing up octopuses that boys picked up alive,
turning them inside-out for sale to restaurants.

STARFISH

No head, five arms and a mouth in the middle
is me on a good day, a day to hunt clams on.
Tally-ho tube-feet, lines of blind will,
march me to the smother of a gathered crush.
Picking through the broken light of the sea-bed,
if anemones surround me I endure downwards.
Doesn't every star? Even the lost ones,
the rolled-up urchins delinquent in the coral,
suck on the darkness of the bottoms they haunt.
I've travelled the light years to scavenge the deep,
budding new courses when arms are bitten off,
their tips curling up to the surface of the sky,
a compass with the added dimension of flesh,
five points jostling for my deep Polaris.

ZEBRA MUSSELS

My love said *Take me away; the Soviet Union*
is packed and poisoned, even her music
unsettles with menace. Dissembled
clouds of our spawn sloshed in the bilges,
every last hull was belly-up to us.
Clamp us on with your big club-foot,
said one of my cunt-faced offspring.
So we held sway through the salted oceans,
a tenacious testament to bivalves.
The new-world opened and the pearl for us
was the glimmering shelves of The Great Lakes.
My love sang sweetly while setting up house,
and we shall lay the blanket of our prickled zest
across this chilled and tender breast.

PORTUGESE MAN O' WAR

No longer the floating menace of the ocean,
my deadly barbs troll floods of junk now.
Drifting with bags that balloon among rafts
of tangled plastic and Styrofoam cups
spilling their sea, we bob a jolly trail
to the north pacific gyre. Swirling
in this Texas-sized mid-ocean toilet
my brushes against living things are rare.
Mostly what my frills touch won't degrade,
though bags break down to minute strands
that infiltrate my tissue like soft bones.
Only a turtle stops to choke down a bag,
or an albatross dips among caps and lighters,
to regurgitate them later to her ravenous young.

TUNA

Racing with dolphins is detrimental
to skipjack tuna that end up canned.
But no fish faster than the bluefin tuna
cuts through water to die on long-lines,
or gets gaffed out of a purse-seine net,
thrashing silver in a blood-red sea.
Some are caught in wandering ghost nets
that sink with the weight of suspended dead,
later to rise up from the dark fathoms,
when their catch has rotted, to snare again.
No more millions swell the high seas,
the last great fish driven like the white whale
by flotillas with Ahab's insatiable will
to consumers incessantly hooked on fine sushi.

FROGS

Park-gate attendants never mention plagues of frogs
leak from the woods under curtains of dusk.
We wondered why campers stayed captive like moths
in the droning halo of the washrooms.
We heard the first pops in the radio silence
after Shostakovich's tin-pan symphony,
his needle to Stalin, puttered to a close.
Slick phantoms slashed our high beams,
wood frogs fired from the ditches,
sounding like pea-pods or plastic package bubbles
when they landed under our tires. Desperate
we scrambled to shoo them away from the road,
cars honked and rolled on relentless as tanks
in light rain slipped the emulsified night.

SNAPPING TURTLE

The roads in Algonquin are salt-licks for moose,
tame as half horses, less jumpy than quarters.
A granny could put her knitting needles aside,
take up a cross-bow and shoot one through the heart.
A bull within yards of us ambles off, leaving
the ditched anger of a snapping turtle to gape
up at its new tormentors. Its pond
across the road is a million miles away.
Another laboured dislocation tells us
this old girl's eggs are laid. Blood etched
across the craggy shell backs up to string
along the road, the road that slices
through domains of turtle and moose. The cut
is clean, the turtle's snapping in two.

SNAKE

I slink through humid gardens like a rumour,
the hint of corruption on tongue-flicked leaves.
Prized among Old Testament phobias,
the deviant phallus that prowls at night.
Well believe me I'd sooner swallow rats
than stalk your daughters. Virgins are not
my particular cup of venom. Buxom Eve,
now there was no lady, when she let the goat loose
the jungle trembled in constriction. The fall
and unceremonious backhand from Eden,
we pay for that, the perfect scapegoats,
skinned alive in your search for devils,
chopped in half for your fear and your conscience...
my tail begins where my neck ends.

TORTOISE
for Nig and Bar

When someone spotted Roger first every dead soldier
rose on his imaginary horse and yee-hawed over.
Even dead Indians were let pick dandelions
to place before the shrunken head before being killed again.
He still trudged when flipped over, someone rubbed
his plastron for rivets. The smell of a hedge-bed
was damp Irish winters in his outside bones.
We knew The Red Sea was just blue in the atlas,
and Egypt was hefty with bones to The Nile,
regions where camels and tortoises trekked,
deliberate pyramids through the blasting desert.
Why then did he always want out of the sandpit,
preferring to criss-cross our own Little-Big-Horns—
small tank to annoy with our practicing arrows?

Dinosaurs

Your heavy step, your cathedral of genes,
remembered in rock, in the oil you've become,
in our cells where your signatures fossilize yet,
that steam-close amphibious scenario percolates.
Backdrops of tree-ferns and gurgling lava,
misplaced extinctions, out-dated life histories...
a layer of theory ashes over the Jurassic.
Time's igneous manner would truncate your eons,
lumbering vats turn swampy, luscious stomachs
cave in empty cold. The small survived,
more tuned to danger than a turn of great necks.
Too late, you envisioned the burrow and the wing,
took one too many meteorites to the jaw,
and died in the gigantic faith of your form.

RAIL

Hold your weight alive, outside to see me,
rail in a cat-tail marsh. Glimpse my halting
stab at a gait. I will appear,
but seldom, like a turtle's breath, so mark
the dash of buffy lavender, the loose bars of my belly,
you think I'm unaware of. Trample like a ton
of grackles towards me and I'll transform
these buoyant footfalls to entangled witches' claws,
and disappear, my blood to flooded dogwood.
I'm mad enough, the marsh wren's rail's incessant,
that sometimes I'd murder a patient God,
seeing the tumbling colours of ducks,
when gunshot cracks the marsh with lead, and I,
small rail against encroachment, shake.

COWBIRDS

We increase, creeping deeper, we're no mothers,
just rude abandoned users of those others,
who lack this monkish stealth in all their colours,
transfixed in the profusion of their songs.
I see their forest fragment under cable,
and we are faster on the heels of men than sparrows,
or this rabble of starlings, who we sit with, for now.
My casual mates throw back their heads, and squeak,
I think of forty eggs to lay in forty nests;
one might be yours, oh my warbling parents,
half my size when finally I was fledged
and gleaned your busy lives around my back.
I'll seek you out, and when you're off the nest,
I'll leave you the egg of your changeling grandchild.

Chicken

When I was jungle-fowl intelligent
colours hid the small fact of my brain,
where I scratched a patch of forest,
and scratched my peers with spurs.
Or gained a hen's eye with sudden ritual,
in the blazing monsoon's orchid chorus.
Now in dumb white slavery to breast
our life-spans crowd a month abreast.
Our wattles clash like angry flags for food,
for hunger that came and tamed us to its knee
and engineered us to these seedless grapes.
If we'd any stuff left...a feather for the flight,
to fill a clearing with new innovation,
to survive the extinction of the upstart ape...

HYACINTH MACAW

Mouthparts like this fit a jungle of nuts...
but here at the zoo we're long in the tooth
and way too blue. Our clown-load of noises
could crack a soprano. Pliers of our keeper
melt in my mouth. My mate's so mean
she's even meaner than me. Throughout March Break,
obnoxious teens brawl for position to reach us,
I climb on my tongue, the black toe of a sailor,
fluff myself out and dare the fuckers to pluck us.
Had they moved us for breeding sooner, my gonads
might have curtailed this cancerous labyrinth
rampant in my liver. I'll die before my chick,
a squawking dollop now, attains our splendid blue
and rises from the rancid mulch of a rum-barrel.

Siberian Crane Dance

I

Here comes that prancing cat's-ass on stilts,
still shaking that stiff Siberian ghost;
it's tied him up in bugle-knots again. He's fixed
his meanest eye on me. His legs will rise,
like high sticks in a marsh, his wings
are racing in short airs of northern warmth.

He's preened and stabbed the beaten air between us.
I've manicured each tension into dance.
At first, a dance stretched-chickens wouldn't dance,
but later lifting the thin angles of our grace
to rest in ruffled white duets, or probe
more tiny tangents of the world into a nest,
that lies like some flung thing between us, hit or miss,
an egg's in the making, our cloacas kiss.

2

If she calls me once more, baldy dagger-head, she's dead.
I'll nail her first, pretend to count my toes,
then rake her plumage out to stomp and fling...
though, for an egg's age now she's bitten back
the urge to bicker, steps have mixed,
her halting gait's become my customary pace.

Bloods unhoused clamour for migration, steady...
the Afghan sky's still shot with careless rapture.
It's here our necks can stretch to chance,
here our demeanour can ease mantled robes
down onto the nest. We'll give skies a miss,
take up water colours, philosophy, mythology we missed.
One learns to love one's wife's long fruity face,
when the future is taken, what's left of us, but grace?

BLACKPOLL WARBLER

If winter scared him down to Argentina,
this half-ounce migrant champion hid it well.
Drab flitter combing leaves...slipped in
and out of shadows from hawks' eyes.
Brushed off the Andes to beef up in Brazil,
on a surfeit of bugs voraciously beaked.
When the season turns inside him like a maggot,
his plumage rises to the fulcrum of his urge.
A cut above Columbia's corrupted jungle,
he dashes on Panama, up the troubled isthmus,
skirting The Gulf, possessed in night skies,
that stride The Great Lakes, homing to the boreal.
When he thumps into my window, dies in my hand,
he's hours short of summer's expanse of black spruce.

King Penguin

Ballistic, the penguins surge ashore,
kings, from a tide embroiled on rocks,
flick desolate reigns of Antarctic seas
off with a quirky two-step. Flat and glibber
than landings under a Shackleton or Scott,
for them it's home, not the abyss.
One egg to be clutched in a two-week blizzard
awaits their attendance. Their dapper forms
to mull over the world's bleak end,
until relief transpires, having plumbed
for weeks, the coldest unknown depths,
for a crop of squid, for a waddled brief
reunion. The fat, furred chick,
to be served to the ends of the earth.

ECHIDNA

Any noise close or a bird's passing shadow
will trigger a flinch...be a quiver of nerves,
ward off all comers with a backful of spines,
in the face of bush-fires just dig down.
Don't ever panic like the platypus did...
swam up a duck's bum, *that* was dodging extinction.
Be careful of love, it's tougher than nails
but the love for a poggle, a mother's love,
that's tender like bellies, like Christ before thorns.
Remember when squeezing eggs out like a reptile,
sweat milk in a pouch like a good little mammal,
and guide the thing in with a beak like no bird's.
Be the oldest most primitive mammal on earth,
make mammy proud, face probing the dirt.

ELEPHANT SHREW

So long clearing detritus from these trails
I'm weary of my own escape routes.
So easily spooked into bounding histrionics
I barely read the scented messages we leave.
Monogamy's one wife too many for me,
and I'm not alone in this, the lot
of an elephant shrew is to forge willy-nilly
along the short tightrope of his life,
nosing the nerves, twitching for cricket-kills.
Given four years before teeth wear out
where's the sense of snapping them at suitors?
Better to be flippant, whiskered desperados,
darting through the ordnance of predetermination,
word of our passage to fade from stick and stone.

MOLE
for Michael

The clouds here were puffs of a toy train, Michael,
God finger-painted that day. That night he untied
the Hale-Bopp comet from the Northwest sky.
Then He strung us along on a lunar eclipse,
to show us He was who He was. You were two,
and a continent away. A star-nosed mole
had died on our ground. Who'd guess,
these storybook creatures keep gruesome larders,
earthworms stashed in little earth spaces,
a nip in the head the anesthetic that keeps them,
as God is ours. Who'd know
that this blind peddler had murderous grace...
Earth-comet led by the star of a nose,
the tail of it, hot tunnel air.

KANGAROO
for Nan Brown

An ocean's vault to close us to this land
cut from me placental mother that most
would leap like refugees from, or be burrowers.
The sun's scorched eye's on the rim of every drought
we pouch our future against, in dry bush that spits venom.
Each marsupial blueprint was read well
by men who caked their skin with dirt and danced
our steps, firing up their laughable dingos.
But you who see me as a deer in a chair, feel free
to make me game beyond your need, or render me
dog-food in the high beams of your sport. You whose
humour's an emu to run me down fence-lines, tell me,
if you lunged in the excellence of the stride that is mine,
would you tear out my leg for a boomerang, man?

HEDGEHOG

When the second Jan fell and found a fiddle in the field
and tore like Stravinsky in a muddied goatee home,
I remembered the first Jan's fall ended eyeball
to eyeball with a wet-nosed Wicklow hedgehog.
"Them fairies" he said, "scooped my concertina,
so I keep these hog for ransom, ja."
These East European musical Jans
top castles for blarney, wink longer,
as jokes sink in translation. That scar
where German bullets hit was *the* perfect excuse
to show my mother his balls. His new
accordion squeezed out hedgehog squeals.
He'd whip it out on every social occasion.
Tense, we bristled, bracing to be poleaxed.

SLOTH

Sometimes the heart sits on every leaf.
Eagles prowl a wing-tip from my reach;
ravenous paws rhyme up the spotted night.
The snappy canopy's no place above an ambush,
so if I dangle scruffy as a jungle armpit,
bug-ridden, toughened to a treetop bum,
who can blame me, and survive on these high streets?
Here where tamanduas cruise, or used to,
too pencil-faced for words, ants by the tongueful
drew them to my tumbled fringes.
But not since men came, and the world
turned haywire, burned and upside down,
too much I'm in water, too much on the ground,
out of my element, ghosting around.

PANGOLIN

Pangolin, tenrec, kinkajou, desman,
tarsier, indri, potto, douroucouli,
bongo, okapi, babarousa, yak,
aye-aye, could go on, binterong and on,
cataloging oddballs, but on a scale of one to ten,
the one with scales would win.
And layers of scales, shingles of horn,
bedeck me. I form the very roof,
that tops the pagoda of mammalian freaks.
Below me is it Hutus clamouring for Tutsis?
Their hearts are dark and empty as their scabbards.
I could be bush-meat, my skin could be slung,
on a Texan dandy unless in chain-mail
I can list through the trees, through the night's inquisition.

BEAVER

When rain had come, un-smoothing what your will
had levelled to a risen pond and still,
we watched you nose the surface of years' work,
as if beneath that tail-flat guidance lurked
some leak or breach to drag your world to edge,
that old, unhurried, busy fear of ledge
stirs in the bear-proof past, untidy lodge
where kits are grooming bundles in the hull,
a little continental underbelly, full
and ripe with broken crosses, winter gnaw,
that rusting snare that left your tail-sides raw.
All courses run their awkward grebe on land,
west opener, just water in the hand
squared your world in feet towards Columbus.

GREY-HEADED FLYING FOX
for Stace

Weeks after your walkabout the fruit-bat still hung there,
shreds of gristle crackling in the hum of the hydro wires.
The grimace of its electric death petrified in a fox's grin.
The locals loved it, gave it high-class roadkill status,
when every pointing tourist drew a gasp at the sight of it.
I saw its thinning cohorts shadow down two centuries,
and pictured Cooke's flamboyant captaincy deflate
when the cat-bark cacophony of crepuscular bickering
unfolded nightmare wings above his head.
Even the numbers were undiscovered. The trees
were lush for scurvy. We remember most
what we don't understand, fragments
torn from the cycle of strange life.
There're swarms of black tents pitched in every memory.

Aardvark

Increasingly I plug my burrow with my body
and come out less willingly to the African night.
When I do, my enemies follow ever closer,
their breath impending, gangs in a frenzy.
Old age is a luxury that comes to nothing here.
One night I'll stumble and they'll tear me to pieces,
fitting for one slapped together, so they say,
from other animals' parts. It's said I'm so ugly
my flesh is delicious, that even queens
are pleased to eat me. I've dug naked mole rats
up, now that's ugly. Too tired to face ant-bites,
I rest on my laurels; the labyrinthine snout,
that has more bones than any other nose,
first place in all good English dictionaries.

SNOWSHOE HARE
for Eric

When I hear a twig snap in the north woods in winter
I want to hop into my snowshoe hare outfit,
stuff my big feet down into the legs,
adjust the ears like antenna for the sounds,
fire up the nose to an incessant twitch,
and electrify each hair so it trembles at the end.
To be able finally to convince my mother,
that I *am* properly dressed for Canadian winters,
and that should a blizzard come pouncing down like a lynx,
or windchill creep up deadlier than owls,
I'd be prepared, and could skedaddle down into my hole—
survival, construed as cowardice by some.
Father, I have changed, no longer a big sissy,
mummy's boy's grown up—I'm a big rabbit now.

BADGER

Days are a nuzzling curl in the sett,
under farm-end hedgerows where I suppose the sun
stifles in the briar, even a finch-hop.
We wait for the dusk, their crackpot logic
doesn't rifle through the ditches then, it stoops
to cozy fires, stokes up idle plans
to smoke us out. As if we've nothing more to do
than snoop around their cattle's ankles
dispensing brucellosis. Heel to snout
we're fog-filled, pack the bandit's eye-wear for evasion,
for night-time passage through the business of need,
to the field's far corner's flare-up of snails,
over gaps and ancient tumbles of stone in old stone walls,
to a future's ever narrowing exposure in the dawn.

RED PANDA

People are faster than ants to swell to heaven,
where I almost am. Their groundless rinse
of rice fields flushes upwards. Hillsides
hacked out, slide to flattened paddies. I'm found
as a rusting sun-ball on the upper groves,
bamboo's green thick whips grow past me.
To keep apace with men I'd need an extra self.
So what damn do I give being lumped with raccoons,
or put less than pandas? When snow gathers on me,
my very thoughts slow to an awkward torpor.
Can one *be* any more indifferent to survival,
when the urge that turns a languid lifestyle frantic
comes but once a year? Love, I smell your day,
and move with a puppet's thick deliverance your way.

WARTHOG

Cobwebs span the jaws where once saliva
glistened. I'm almost sorry for that leopard.
We stared each other down so long, our plaques
against our walls. They took us down
for giving children nightmares. The gerenuk too,
though him for popping seams. Three heads junked
in a mansion's attic where generations of maids,
who rubbed dust off our eyes, once slept.
Propped on crooked tusks among old insults;
the Bwana holds my hacked-off head in photos,
while natives fling the rest of me to crocs;
bills from a taxidermist who tossed me from a taxi;
museums' polite refusals to offers of my sale.
My end lives on in the junk of a has-been.

MUSK OX

I keep my hook-ended bonnet on tight
in case of a lanky ambush of wolves.
Behind it, the reinforced skull of a goat
is for the rivalry, for when we charge
like clansmen, full belt, skirts to the wind,
into each other's heads. The dull clack,
like coconuts over the Barrens, skims the eskers,
enters the hollow bones of birds, becomes the torn
sandpiper cry. This is either the top
or the end of the world. Sometimes I teeter,
expecting an edge to the loosening thaw.
Other times we stand a week in a blizzard,
a cluster of dullards, like rugs draped over
items of furniture abandoned to the cold.

Zebra

Long white lines of us straggle the veld.
The dry season's trek between water and dust
is done. Clouds dash in patterns of thunder
and stoke the foals up. Catching whiffs
of passing lions sends shudders up our manes.
Deadened in the heat, we mares graze on...
Stallion-banter, the whinny of a jack-ass
dips in a tango of bites and high hooves.
Everywhere gazelles are pronking
as if the ground gives off electric shocks.
Sisters, I'm frisky. Our daily brush with death
is still ahead...We'll turn as one,
lightening hocks to a blur of streaks,
my full rump rounding into the gallop.

HIPPO

Along the river-bottom the big-bottomed denizens
bouncing so lightly they could be moon-hippos,
come into their own and park in the eddies.
Rainy seasons come here like good times that roll
like crocodiles at a carcass. Babies are born
and bubble at the surface. Fish knife
through the risen river, the lounge of level heads,
where knobble-eyed males fly off now and then
in backhoe-mouthed rages. At night they plod
to hippo lawns, mouths low and leading,
sweeping slow across each step, divining
what's below, water for the shrinking days,
the dry season's prospectus, it's pull of mud,
weighing heavy on their heads.

Rhino

Excessive enterprise and then excessive rest
is how gods work. In seven days a world...
then zilch for twenty million more.
But blue, the great back aching constant want,
arched over rifty Africa for soothing,
God, mustering His toughest rubber, summoned rhino,
bound him, horn-tight, trundle to the dusty hilt,
cantankerous rhino, snorty for the dagger-heave.

A leopard drops a buckled antelope to jackals;
halfway up giraffes' necks cud stalls;
ears everywhere flick oxpeckers off.
What issues from the distant lopped Acacias,
where the haze of God-breath shakes for lack of rhino?
Wheeled fleets are combing bush for tamer game.

HYENA

On TV we always get bit parts with vultures,
trundling round a bickered kill, blood stuck
to half our coats like angry jam. To take a leg
and run, for half the scruff in Africa to chase,
makes for essential Serengeti footage.
Some glamorous profiles of felines have us
panting hot wind that ruffles lazy manes...
a galloping appetite outflanking itself,
in wayward lurches, giddy gnashing jaw-snaps.
The plain's dynamic heaves beyond impressions,
a million years we've sniffed its herded pulse,
butcher than dogs, our beefed up she-men run,
on pure testosterone among the glut of calves,
maternity churning out their episodic deaths.

BLACK BEAR

That pig-eyed black glance crashing bush
swallowed from a clearing, sure made our hearts gulpy.
Surprise a bear upwind and anything
can happen. If there were cubs or kids I could wife,
settle our differences with a paw-swipe.
But bedrock punching back the heat
takes the muscled ripple of a stumpy canter
up another ridge. Around here Grandpa Cutts
disappeared, they found his dinted blueberry pail
empty. Swamp pockets the Shield here, feeds
the soggy tundra, streams of our diminished trails.
Men lost in personal, calculated fear un-sling
rifles over seedy scat and stalk black bear,
sow or boar, damned for a bladder of gall.

Snow Leopard

A wisp in high gaps one breath away,
a chimera gone into cloud, snow leopard,
patrolling where weather can hurl itself down
on a whim of scree to freezing torrents.
Laid up on some Promethean ledge,
green flames burning for ibex or markor,
till famished resolve cracked, and he settled
for marmot or mouse. Now in the fleece
of a winter storm he descends into valleys,
a ghost driven down into human haunts.
He will tender provisions of caution to hunger,
slinking in meadows of dangerous scent.
The bleats of wild-eyed domestics will huddle,
cries to be stifled in the risk of his hide.

GREY SEAL
for Brendan

Surf brims. Our teenage sons fixate on shore. You'd swear
by their bobbing gawks we hanker after the quick
toes of the land. Not so, and bash me on a Blasket
if I'm wrong, but it's the tidal plunge
of a rut-bull, anchors them out like blinking buoys.
Pupped on Ireland's Eye, our wet gangs used to bask
like dog-arsed larvae on the honeycombed Antrim basalt.
These days, mooching harbours for offal,
grow murky with ease. Far rougher a flounder,
flat as a flipper, taken in the breakers,
munch its scrunchy face in the lick of a whisker.
Also, for pig-iron, we'd wait under currachs
as lobster-pots lowered like baskets of prayers,
saying, take from the sea all the offered surf brims with.

Sea Cows

Frequently propellers cleave into the flesh
of some big lush that lolls in a lagoon,
then the blood of a mermaid tumbles on a lek,
like a siren leaking and the manatees scatter.
No tide's safe now, sea-grass falters
in the heaving wash, sea cows graze
where anchors snag the verges. From deeper
where the sea-bed bottoms out in caverns,
where sharks hone their noses on the dim brine,
red tide sucks its toxins to the shallows.
Their coastlines melted in palls of luxury,
elephantine dolphin-women recede like the hulls
of ghost-ships downwards, history is quickening,
extravagant indifference gushes from the bilges.

Elephants

I
Africa 1970

Matriarchal trumpeting summons their attention.
Ears flapped out, they rumble to the circle
of a herd standing fast. One bellows at the bush.
Something's not right, trunks in the air
try to siphon it out. Calves disappear
in the dusty agitation. Wave after wave
of wildebeest drown the infra-sound
of a bull in musth. Even estrous
cows decipher something other
than his coming. In a haze of hormones,
crimped and magisterial, Africa's shoulder,
glides on the pronged rack of his will,
ignoring the impalas erupting from the bush,
where the glint of sudden metal flashes like a leopard.

2

I see them unloaded at the orphanage, traumatized,
suffering mock charges and trunk shots
from bigger residents. Their benefactors,
hosing death off them to alleviate the stink,
all awash again in the plains' prodigious caking,
panic returning as the watered blood of mothers
runs once more down their sides. One is calm,
a sickly one whose trunk drops half the stones
she's throwing on her back. Diarrhea
splashes her heels. A budding tusk promises
to veer forever left. The new arrivals,
adjusting to lawless juvenile confinement,
charge against the fence on the far side of which,
bones of their families bleach Mozambique.

3
CANADA 2005

Each one in order waits their turn to enter.
Through ports the grey ocean of their bulk
teem before the doors. They look out whales' eyes,
checking the cables and gates with their trunks,
then proceed through the lock-up routine of the day.
Tessa's last in, left tusk points away
as if redirecting unwanted attentions
from cohorts and keepers. Having spent
thirty years at the zoo baffling the vets,
only the other six elephants seem unsurprised
she's still alive. They mostly ignore her,
have their own agendas. Their place within the herd
dictating their behaviour. Their ivory's set,
chess pieces moving on the board of our making.

RIGHT WHALE

We're always leaving, and our young,
enormous mollusks, fasten to our sides.
Their hugs are currents, guidance is the moon
that pulls the girdles of the world. We dive
down into gulfs, long windows, dreams,
not just the swallowed-sailor type, but stretching
from the mud of creatures, necks
and fangs, new fangled, flashing in the air,
for blood's ancestry, forcing toeholds there...
and the return, unfisting here to fluke...
Air calls the lungs, the nostrils on the head
from each black fathom. Its reluctant dependents
plunge out, unhoisted, our mark upon the earth
is the wallop of old boots on the Atlantic.

GIBBON

Frayed silhouettes of bats chatter in the dawn
or drip in the mist. The mangroves breathe.
The day's hung gambled on a gibbon's wrist
as the greens take shape and the inaccessible enclaves
ring with the bucolic whoops of a male
who's ambushing the air with leaps of total faith,
a little bishop bare-faced up a lush Vatican.
His mate's got the puckered look of a nun down pat.
She runs along a hung teak bough
like that napalmed Vietnamese girl in the picture
that helped end the war. Gravity,
as if it were pain or sin, shakes from the flesh,
plunges in a beading neckline of the forest,
an angel glancing off the handles of the world.

CHIMPANZEE
for Sue

Our Christmas Eve family rituals grew cultish
as midnight closed us tight round sisters' gifts.
Lucky for you we received Sonny that day,
so were otherwise engaged. African heirlooms
shifting in mahogany irises...the shaky look
of a six-month-orphaned chimpanzee.
He'd cling so tight it pinched. We Irish held
one referendum after the next. Abortion, divorce...
knuckling down to tribalism again. Given our time
to raise and ready him for life in the zoo,
the unwanted unborns and the dicey marriages
would still be intact in the minds of the righteous.
Was it that he was too close, almost us, or that
his cage-mates were, that he ended up drowned in the moat?

Notes

Cuchulain

Cuchulain is an iconic figure from Irish mythology whose heroic qualities became symbolic for the Gaelic Revival of the early twentieth century.

Like the heroes of classical Greece, he prevailed against massive odds and engaged in superhuman feats such as fighting the sea. When finally he succumbed in battle, mortally wounded by his enemies, he lashed his disemboweled body to a rock so he would remain upright. His enemies, afraid to approach while he still lived, waited until a raven landed on his shoulder before they came close. A statue depicting this scene stands in the General Post Office in Dublin.

Armada

In the autumn of 1588 the scattered galleons of the first Spanish Armada, after being defeated by the English fleet at Gravelines, were being pounded by storms all along the west coast of Ireland. Some sixty ships were wrecked, their crews drowning or struggling ashore to an unpredictable reception from the Irish. They were as likely to be dispatched for their clothing as to be sheltered for their common religious faith and anti-English intentions.

Rhino Keeper
The narrator of this poem employs the syntax and thick accent particular to the "north side" of Dublin. Corus Iompar Eireann is the national public transport company.

Moving Statues
Ballinspittle, a small village in County Cork, was home to a particularly animated statue of the Virgin Mary in 1985.

Lough Derg
"Midgets" is a common malapropism for midges (tiny pestilent flies) in Ireland.

Indian Summer.
In 1812, Thomas Douglas, Earl of Selkirk, received a vast land grant from the Hudson's Bay Company surrounding the confluence of the Red and Assiniboine Rivers where Winnipeg is situated today. His aim was to establish a Scottish colony there. By 1815, three hundred and fifty Scots had made the grueling journey through the difficult country of the Canadian Shield, following the maze of waterways and portages used by the *voyageurs* and fur traders before them. "Crowduck" is a Scottish term for cormorants which breed in huge numbers along with pelicans on the northern basin of Lake Winnipeg.

Wounded Knee.
In December of 1890, on hearing that Sitting Bull had been killed, a gravely ill Chief Big Foot and his band of three hundred Minneconjou Sioux, fearing for their lives, fled Standing Rock to seek protection at the Pine Ridge Agency. The destitute group of mainly women and children were intercepted north of Wounded Knee by a detachment of five hundred troops of the U.S. 7th Cavalry. After a night encamped under guard, the band was ordered to surrender all weapons. A couple of warriors refused to give their guns up, a shot went off, and in the general panic, the surrounding troops opened fire with their Hotchkiss guns. More than one hundred and forty Indians were killed. Relations between the 7th Cavalry and the Sioux had been incendiary since the debacle of Little Big Horn fourteen years before.

In 1975 two F.B.I. agents and a Native American were killed during a botched raid on the Pine Ridge reservation near Wounded Knee. Leonard Peltier was convicted of murder on the basis that his red pick-up truck was on the scene the day of the shootings. He is still imprisoned in what is widely considered one of the greatest travesties of justice in U.S. history.

It is believed that Crazy Horse's heart is buried at Wounded Knee.

Meet the Hairy-Nosed Wombat Keeper
The Southern Hairy-Nosed Wombat is an endangered marsupial less well known than its close relative, the common wombat.

Zebra Mussels
A prolific Eurasian mollusk inadvertently released in the Great Lakes in the 1980s probably with the bilge water of cargo ships. Like many introduced species, their presence has enormously damaged certain native ecosystems.

Tuna
Unsustainable fishing practices have reduced populations of all the oceans' great fisheries by 90% in the last fifty years.

Cowbirds
Brown-headed cowbirds are brood parasites that have extended their range enormously as a consequence of people clearing the once ubiquitous woodlands of the eastern half of this continent. This expansion of the range of the cowbird has come largely at the expense of the various warbler species and other songbirds who frequently end up raising the larger more aggressive cowbird chicks instead of their own. Woodland species are more susceptible than grassland species, the latter having built up various strategies of resistance over thousands of generations of exposure to the practice.

Siberian Crane Dance
Siberian cranes are one of the most endangered birds on earth. This poem is inspired by a visit to the International Crane Foundation in Wisconsin, where these and other species of cranes are bred for re-introduction to the wild whenever that course of action is feasible.

Blackpoll Warbler
It has been estimated that a million songbirds die every day on this continent alone as a result of collisions with glass.

Echidna
The short-beaked echidna or spiny anteater is one of only three species comprising the order of Monotremes. The duck-billed platypus is another of these primitive and shy egg-laying mammals. Poggle is the term for a baby monotreme.

Pangolin
The pangolin or scaly anteater is the only mammal to have scales like a reptile. An arboreal recluse, this species is under increasing pressure from the bush-meat trade, an illegal activity that is decimating wildlife in central Africa.

Badger
In Ireland the Eurasian badger is considered to be a carrier/vector of brucellosis, and as such has been widely persecuted there.

Red Panda
The red or lesser panda is a smaller cousin of the hugely popular giant panda, the international symbol of endangered animals. Like its cuddly relative, this species has been classified in various orders over the years as biologists argued over where it belonged. Both types of panda are specialized to such a degree that fragmentation of their habitats could be detrimental to their survival. Their breeding strategies seem particularly limiting, females being receptive for only one or two days a year. These animals can enter a sort of mini-hibernation during cold snaps.

Zebra
Pronking is a form of stiff-legged jumping commonly displayed by smaller antelopes.

Hyena
Female spotted hyenas are larger and more aggressive than males. Testosterone levels are indistinguishable between the sexes. This adaptation has evolved in response to the fierce competition for food within clans of hyenas.

Black Bear
Worldwide, bears are killed for their gallbladders, for which there is a lucrative black market, and which are believed by factions of eastern medicine to contain healing and or aphrodisiac powers.

Sea Cow
Manatees and dugongs form the order Sirenia, an unassuming group that ironically occupies a powerful presence in folklore and mythology. These are the mermaids of seafarers and the Sirens that lured Ulysses and his band on their return from Troy. Each year many manatees die or are injured as a result of being hit by outboard motor propellers. Another more recent and insidious threat to these endangered creatures is red tide, a phenomena that occurs from time to time as excess nutrients from human activities and farming practices build up to toxic levels in the ocean and suddenly choke stretches of coastline.

Grey Seal
The Blasket Islands lie off the Dingle peninsula in Kerry. They once supported a thriving community of Irish-speaking fishermen and their families. Ireland's Eye is a small island off the coast of Dublin. The honeycombed Antrim basalt is the famous Giants Causeway in County Antrim. A currach is a traditional rowboat used extensively along the west coast of Ireland during the last two centuries.

ACKNOWLEDGEMENTS

For their encouragement and friendship over the years it has taken to produce this book, I am grateful to David Partington, Charles Guthrie and Brendan Price. To Paul Vermeersch, my editor, whose confidence in the original manuscript inspired me to write what turned out to be some of my favourite poems in the book. To my family, Irish and Canadian, this would not be what it is without you.